C000244429

DIESELS IN NORTH & MID WALES

Trenau Diesel yng Ngogledd a Chanolbarth Cymru

On Sunday 31st May 1987, Class 47/4 No. 47639 *Industry Year 1986* passes Bangor signal box, as it approaches the station with a Holyhead to Euston train. In the background can be seen the entrance to Belmont Tunnel with its "Egyptian" style portico.

John Hillmer

One of the dedicated fleet of 'Railfreight Metals' locomotives based at Canton, No. 37901 *Mirrlees Pioneer,* passes Ruabon with the 11.30 'special' from Dee Marsh Junction to Margam (6Z42) on 26th September 1987. The load is 22 empty BBA and BAA steel coil wagons.

Paul Shannon

DIESELS IN NORTH & MID WALES

Trenau Diesel yng Ngogledd a Chanolbarth Cymru

John Hillmer & Paul Shannon

Oxford Publishing Co.

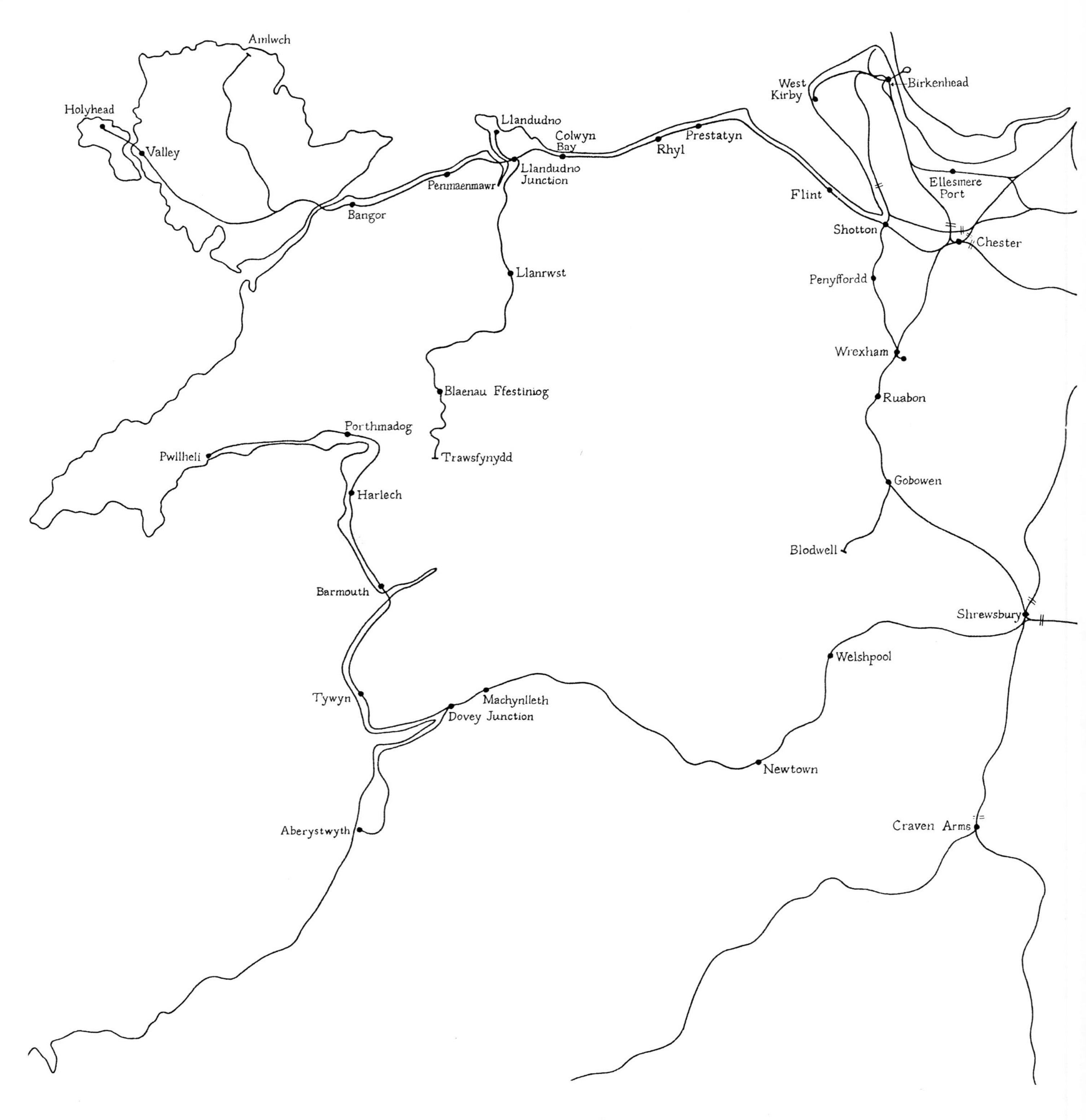

A FOULIS-OPC Railway Book

British Library Cataloguing in Publication Data
Hillmer, John
Diesels in North & Mid Wales.
1. Wales. Railway services. Diesel locomotives, history
I. Title II. Shannon, Paul
625.26109429

ISBN 0-86093-427-6

Library of Congress catalog card number
90-81745

Published by:
Haynes Publishing Group
Sparkford, Near Yeovil, Somerset. BA22 7JJ

Haynes Publications Inc.
861 Lawrence Drive, Newbury Park, California 91320, USA.

Printed by J.H. Haynes & Co. Ltd

Introduction

The area covered in this album includes some of the most beautiful scenery in the British Isles, from the delightfully green and gentle Conwy Valley to the stark slate-covered mountains of Blaenau Ffestiniog, from the busy holiday resorts of Colwyn Bay and Rhyl to the peaceful stretches of rocky coastline north of the Dovey Estuary. The railway environment, too, is full of interest, even though many rural lines have disappeared from the map altogether in the last 25 years. Whilst mechanical signalling remains well in evidence along the North Wales Coast and between Shrewsbury and Wrexham, with both upper and lower quadrant semaphores still in use, they are gradually being replaced by colour lights. Other railway features, such as viaducts and station buildings, give interesting insights into the history of the lines that they decorate.

Although neither city is in the Principality, we felt that both Chester and Shrewsbury should be included, as each forms a rail "gateway" into Wales.

For many years the traction scene in North and Mid Wales was dominated by locomotives of Classes 24, 25, 40 and 45, all of which have now been withdrawn from BR service. Nowadays most locomotive-hauled trains in our area are entrusted to that highly successful and versatile machine, the Class 47. But other types also make regular appearances, such as the Class 37s on Cambrian passenger services and Classes 20, 31, 37 and 56 on a variety of freight workings. One extant type which no longer appears is the Class 33, which for a time operated "through" Cardiff to Bangor or Holyhead trains. As in many parts of the BR system, 'Sprinter' units of Class 150/1, 150/2 and 156 have taken over the majority of local passenger workings, though first-generation diesel multiple units have by no means been ousted altogether.

Virtually the only remaining locomotive-hauled passenger trains on the North Wales coast line are the Euston services. The number of summer Saturday extras to the North Wales Coast has declined in recent years, as BR can no longer afford to allocate so many resources to purely seasonal work. However, on the Cambrian, the daily Aberystwyth to Euston train is augmented on summer Saturdays to three, together with two from Pwllheli. "Sprinters" provide through services from the North Wales Coast to Cardiff, Crewe, Manchester and Stalybridge, where passengers can change for direct trains to Hull, Scarborough or Newcastle, each destination having been served in previous years by through services from North Wales. It is good to see several stations re-opened between Chester and Holyhead, the latest being at Conwy in 1987 while Holyhead station is to receive new passenger facilities to replace those demolished some years ago.

Freight traffic in North Wales is conveyed on a mixture of Freightliner, company and Speedlink services. Holyhead Container Terminal is linked by daily trains to London, Cardiff and Birmingham, as well as a connecting service to Crewe for other destinations. Company trains carry petroleum coke to Holyhead (Anglesey Aluminium), chemicals to and from Amlwch (Associated Octel), nuclear flasks from Valley and Trawsfynydd, and coal from North Wales' last rail-connected pit, Point of Ayr. Most of the stone from Penmaenmawr is ballast for BR's own use, but a new revenue earning service to Ashburys, Manchester started during 1987, and on Fridays during the late 1980s a visit was made by two Class 37s hauling a rake of PHAs from the Peak Forest to Washwood Heath circuit, forming an additional working from Penmaenmawr to Salford. Further east, steel coil is sent to BSC Shotton in trainloads from Ravenscraig, Llanwern and Port Talbot, and Penyffordd cement works despatches a block train to Oakengates up to twice a week. For smaller consignments of freight, Speedlink trains operate from Warrington to Llandudno Junction and Dee Marsh Junction, whilst terminals around Shrewsbury are served from Bescot. Llandudno Junction in turn is the starting point for "trips" to Holyhead and until 1988 a terminal at Maentwrog Road near Trawsfynydd Power Station. Traffic conveyed by Speedlink includes aluminium from Holyhead, cement to Bangor, coal and oil to Llandudno Junction, timber to Shotton, timber to Chirk, scrap from Shotton, cement to and from Penyffordd, steel from Wrexham, and oil to Shrewsbury.

An interesting flow of timber from Roman Bridge, on the Conwy Valley line, was in prospect in 1990. Gobowen is the mosy unlikely destination for a thrice-weekly Speedlink Coal service from Washwood Heath, also conveying traffic for Shrewsbury. The Blodwell branch remained in use until 1988 for a daily ballast train to Bescot. On Cambrian lines, freight traffic between Machynlleth and Pwllheli ceased upon the temporary closure of Barmouth Bridge in the early 1980s, but Aberystwyth still receives a weekly petroleum train from Stanlow.

The prospects for the 1990s are good. Certainly the improved A55 trunk road will bring increased competition for BR's passenger services along the North Wales Coast, but BR is confident that it can respond with further improvements to its own services. There is even the possibility of electrification to Holyhead, if suitable funding can be obtained. Many of the freight flows mentioned above have a stable future and it is possible that a new flow of liquid sulphur to Amlwch will have started by the time this book appears in print. All in all, the new decade should prove to hold as much interest for the enthusiast as the decade which produced most of the photographs in this book.

In conclusion, we should like to thank the many BR employees who have kindly supplied information and the contributing photographers who have allowed us to make use of their work, and especially Wyn Hobson to whom we are also indebted for the Welsh translations. We hope that the reader finds as much pleasure in our pictorial record as we have had in compiling it.

Paul Shannon and John Hillmer

Rhagymadrodd

Mae'r ardal yr ymdrinir â hi yn y gyfrol hon yn cynnwys rhai o olygfeydd mwyaf trawiadol gwledydd Prydain. Ceir yma fwynder hyfryd ac iraidd Dyffryn Conwy, a gerwinder mynyddoedd a thomennydd llechi Blaenau Ffestiniog; prysurdeb cyrchfannau gwyliau Bae Colwyn a'r Rhyl, a hedd y morlin creigiog sy'n dirwyn hyd lan ogleddol aber Afon Dyfi. Llawn diddordeb, hefyd, yw byd rheilffyrdd y rhanbarth, er gwaethaf diflaniad sawl lein wledig oddi ar y map dros y chwarter canrif diwethaf. Tra bod rhywfaint o signalu mecanyddol yn parhau ar hyd lein arfordir y Gogledd, a rhwng yr Amwythig a Wrecsam, gyda semafforau cwadrant-uwch a chwadrant-is yn dal mewn defnydd, mae signalau golau-lliw yn graddol gymryd eu lle. Ceir nodweddion eraill, hefyd, fel pontydd ac adeiladau gorsafoedd, sydd yn taflu goleuni diddorol ar hanes y rheilffyrdd y maent yn addurn arnynt.

Er bod y ddwy dref yn gorwedd y tu hwnt i'r ffin, teimlasom mai priodol fyddai cynnwys ymdriniaeth â Chaer a'r Amwythig yn y gyfrol, gan eu bod ill dwy yn ffurfio 'pyrth mynediad' i Gymru.

Am flynyddoedd lawer, injans o Ddosbarthiadau 24, 25, 40 a 45 oedd amlycaf ar wasanaethau yng Ngogledd a Chanolbarth Cymru. Bellach, dilëwyd y Dosbarthiadau hyn, ac erbyn heddiw y mae mwyafrif y trenau a dynnir gan injans yn nwylo'r peiriannau llwyddiannus ac amryddawn hynny, Dosbarth 47. Fodd bynnag, gwelir mathau eraill o injan yn gyson hefyd, gan gynnwys injans Dosbarth 37 ar rai o drenau Lein y Cambrian, ac injans o Ddosbarthiadau 20, 31, 37 a 56 ar amrywiaeth o drenau nwyddau. Un teip o injan sydd yn bod o hyd ond na welir bellach yng Nghymru yw Dosbarth 33, a fu'n gweithio trenau o Gaerdydd i Fangor neu Gaergybi am gyfnod.

Fel sydd yn wir am rannau helaeth o rwydwaith Rh. P., trenau 'Sprinter' o Ddosbarthiadau 150/1, 150/2 a 156 a welir ar fwyafrif y trenau teithwyr lleol bellach - er na ddisodlwyd y genhedlaeth gyntaf o unedau diesel yn gyfan gwbl o bell fordd. Erbyn hyn, y gwasanaethau i Euston yw ymron yr unig drenau teithwyr a dynnir gan injans ar lein Arfordir y Gogledd. Bu lleihad, dros y blynyddoedd diwethaf, yn nifer y trenau ychwanegol a redir i arfordir y Gogledd ar Sadyrnau o haf, gan na all Rh. P. bellach fforddio neilltuo cymaint o adnoddau ar gyfer gwaith sydd o natur tymhorol yn unig. Ar Lein y Cambrian, fodd bynnag, ychwanegir at y gwasanaeth dyddiol rhwng Aberystwyth ac Euston gan ddau drên ychwanegol, ynghyd â dau o Bwllheli i Euston, ar Sadyrnau rhwng misoedd Mai a Medi.

Gan drenau 'Sprinter' y darperir y gwasanaethau o Ogledd Cymru i Gaerdydd, Crewe, Manceinion a Stalybridge (lle gall teithwyr newid i drenau i Hull, Scarborough neu Newcastle - trefi a wasanaethid mewn blynyddoedd a fu gan drenau uniongyrchol o Ogledd Cymru). Da yw gweld ail-agor sawl gorsaf rhwng Caer a Chaergybi - y diweddaraf yng Nghonwy ym 1987 - a bwriedir darparu cyfleusterau newydd ar gyfer teithwyr yng ngorsaf Caergybi, i gymryd lle'r rhai a ddymchwelwyd rai blynyddoedd yn ôl.

Cludir traffig nwyddau rheilffyrdd Gogledd Cymru mewn cymysgedd o wasanaethau 'Freightliner', 'Speedlink' a threnau cwmni. Cysylltir terfynell amlwythi Caergybi â Llundain, Caerdydd a Birmingham gan drenau dyddiol, ac y mae hefyd wasanaeth 'cyswllt' i Crewe ar gyfer cyrchfannau eraill. Ceir trenau cwmni i gludo golosg petrolewm i Gaergybi (Aliwminiwm Môn), cemegolion i Amlwch (Associated Octel) ac hefyd oddi yno, fflasgiau niwclear o'r Fali a Thrawsfynydd, a glo o'r Parlwr Du, y lofa olaf yng Nglogledd Cymru sydd â chyswllt â'r rheilffordd. Ar ffurf balast at ddefnydd Rh. P. eu hunain yw'r rhan fwyaf o'r llwythi gwenithfaen a gludir o Benmaenmawr; ond cychwynwyd gwasanaeth masnachol newydd i Ashburys, Manceinion, yn ystod 1987, ac ar ambell Ddydd Gwener ar ddiwedd y 1980au, ceid ymweliad gan ddwy injan o Ddosbarth 37 ar drên o wagenni PHA (a oedd yn arfer gweithio'r gwasanaeth rhwng chwarel Peak Forest a Washwood Heath, ger Birmingham), er mwyn ffurfio gwasanaeth ychwanegol o Benmaenmawr i Salford.

I'r dwyrain, cludir coil dur i waith Dur Prydain yn Shotton mewn trenau o Ravenscraig, Llanwern a Phorth Talbot, ac anfonir trên cyflawn hyd at ddwywaith yr wythnos o waith sment Penyffordd i Oakengates, Sir Amwythig. Ar gyfer llwythi llai o nwyddau, darperir trenau 'Speedlink' o Warrington i Gyffordd Llandudno, Y Waun, a Chyffordd Wern Dyfrdwy, a gwasanaethir terfynellau ardal Yr Amwythig gan drenau o Bescot, ger Wolverhampton. Anfonir trenau byrion o nwyddau ymlaen o Gyffordd Llandudno i Gaergy bi, a hyd at 1988 anfonid trenau cyffelyb i derfynell ger hen orsaf Maentwrog Road, ar bwys atomfa Trawsfynydd.

Mae'r nwyddau a gludir ar drenau 'Speedlink' yn cynnwys aliwminiwm o Gaergybi, sment i Fangor, glo ac olew i Gyffordd Llandudno, coedwydd i Shotton a'r Waun, haearn sgrap o Shotton, sment i Benyffordd ac hefyd oddi yno, dur o Wrecsam, ac olew i'r Amwythig. Erbyn 1990, yr oedd rhagolygon diddorol hefyd ar gyfer cychwyn gwasanaeth cludo coedwydd o ardal gorsaf Roman Bridge, ar lein Dyffryn Conwy. Gobowen (coelied neu beidio) yw cyrchnod gwasanaeth glo 'Speedlink' sy'n rhedeg deirgwaith yr wythnos o Washwood Heath, gan gludo nwyddau i'r Amwythig yn ogystal. Parheid i ddefnyddio'r lein i Lanyblodwel hyd at 1988, ar gyfer trên balast dyddiol i Bescot. Ar Lein y Cambrian, rhoddwyd y gorau i'r gwasanaeth nwyddau rhwng Machynlleth a Phwllheli pan gaewyd Pont y Bermo dros dro, ar ddechrau'r 1980au, ond y mae terfynell Aberystwyth yn parhau i dderbyn trên petrolewm wythnosol o Stanlow, Swydd Gaer.

Mae'r rhagolygon ar gyfer y 1990au yn dda. Mae'n wir y bydd gwasanaethau teithwyr Rh. P. ar hyd arfordir y Gogledd yn wynebu cystadleuaeth galetach yn sgîl y gwelliannau i ffordd yr A55, ond mae Rh. P. yn hyderus y gallant ymateb gyda gwelliannau pellach i'r gwasanaethau hynny. Y mae posibilrwydd, hyd yn oed, o drydaneiddio'r lein i Gaergybi, pe gellid trefnu'r cyllid priodol. Mae dyfodol diogel i lawer o'r gwasanaethau nwyddau a grybwyllwyd uchod, ac y mae posibilrwydd y bydd gwasanaeth newydd i gludo sylffwr hylif i Amlwch wedi cychwyn erbyn y cyhoeddir y llyfr hwn. Drwodd a thro, dylai'r ddegawd nesaf brofi'n llawn mor ddiddorol i selogion y rheilffyrdd â'r ddegawd a gynhyrchodd y rhan fwyaf o'r lluniau a welir yn y gyfrol hon.

I gloi, hoffem ddiolch am garedigrwydd y llu o weithwyr Rh. P. a ddarparodd wybodaeth ar ein cyfer, a'r ffotograffwyr a ganiataodd i ni wneud defnydd o'u gwaith, yn arbennig felly Wyn Hobson, a fu hefyd ya gyfrifol am gyfieithu'r Rhagymadrodd. Gobeithiwn y caiff y darllenydd gymaint o bleser wrth bori drwy'r cofnod darluniadol hwn ag a gawsom ninnau wrth ei gasglu ynghyyd.

Paul Shannon a John Hillmer

(cyfieithiad: Wyn Hobson)

Early Diesel Days 1 – North Wales Coast

Class 24 No. D5085 leaves Llandegai Tunnel with the daily 'up' halides train from Associated Octel at Amlwch, on 24th April 1967.

Wyn Hobson

On 7th September 1961, a four-car "Derby lightweight" formation, in original green livery, heads east by Penmaen Head with the 'up' "Welsh dragon".

I.G. Holt

Bearing the "lion and wheel" emblem, Type 4 English Electric No. D338 approaches Colwyn Bay with the Holyhead to Euston "Irish Mail" on 7th September 1967.

I.G. Holt

Double-headed Class 25s were a regular feature in North Wales on summer Saturdays. In this picture, Nos D7511 and D7561 are arriving at Llandudno Junction with the 08.36 (SO) Nottingham (Midland) to Llandudno on 2nd July 1966.
Wyn Hobson

A Derby Class 108 diesel multiple unit stands in one of the bays at Llandudno Junction, with a Llandudno branch working on 4th June 1966.
Wyn Hobson

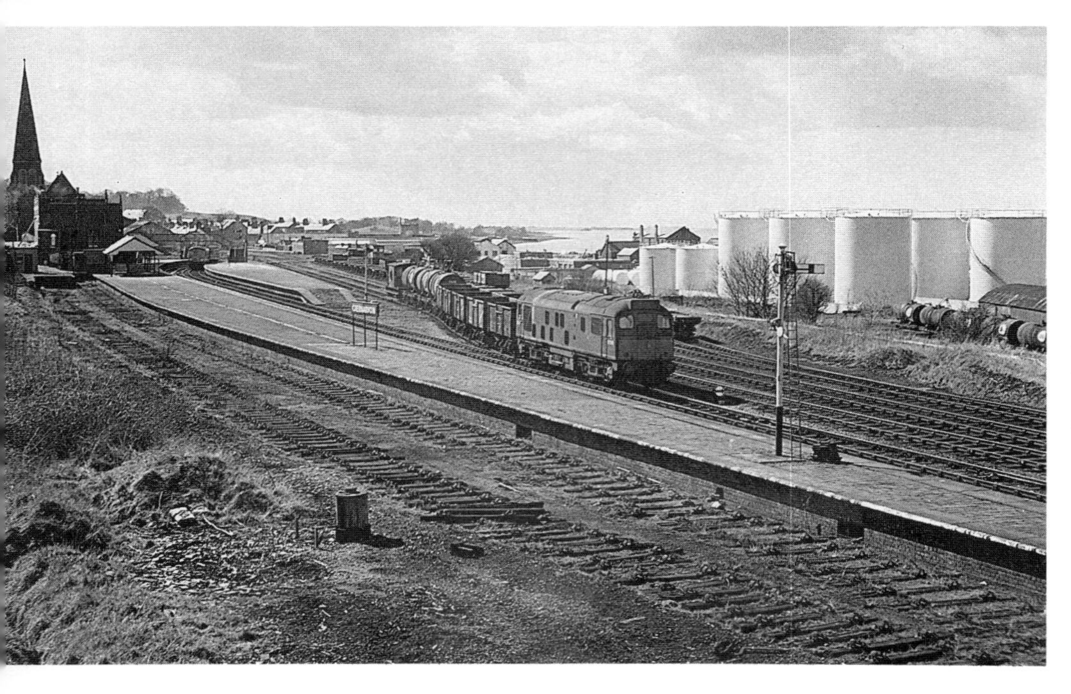

Class 24/1 No. D5145 leaves Caernarvon with the twice- weekly freight on 1st April 1969. No. D5080 is in the background with an inspection coach. The line from Bangor to Caernarvon closed to freight in 1969 and to passenger workings early in 1970, only to be re-opened between June 1970 and February 1972 for a temporary Freightliner terminal in place of Holyhead, whilst the Britannia Bridge was being rebuilt.
Wyn Hobson

On 31st March 1967, Class 24 No. D5077 leaves Caernarvon with the 'up' branch freight, consisting largely of BR design cattle wagons.

Wyn Hobson

Class 47 No. 1818 at the temporary Freightliner depot by the closed Caernarvon station on New Year's Day 1971, during the period when the main line to Holyhead was closed following the Britannia Bridge fire.

Wyn Hobson

Anglesey

Class 47 No. 47571 has brought in the 07.55 from Coventry on 16th June 1988. Class 08 No. 08921 took out the stock and is seen putting it through the washing plant, having released the train locomotive which will leave Holyhead with the 13.05 "Irish Mail" to Euston. In the background the *St Columba* has arrived on the morning sailing from Dun Laoghaire. In July 1988 the contract was signed between Sealink, BR and Anglesey Borough Council for a £23m joint venture of a new station complex.

John Hillmer

'Pacer' No. 142066 leaves from the other side of Holyhead station, on 16th June 1988, forming the 12.00 to Llandudno. To the right (off picture) is the Freightliner Terminal which handles container traffic to and from Ireland. Trains leave on weekdays for London (Stratford and Willesden), Birmingham (Lawley Street), Cardiff (Pengam) and Crewe (for connection with other trunk services).

John Hillmer

Class 47 No. 47536 clatters over the points and crossings as it reaches its destination with the 12.40 London Euston- Holyhead service on 17th April 1985. The terminus retained its mechanical signalling in 1988, including the intricate point rodding visible in the bottom right-hand corner of this photograph.

Paul Shannon

The 12.46 Holyhead to Manchester Victoria, formed of two two-car Class 101 dmu sets, passes the old steam shed on 7th July 1985. A Class 120 unit is in the depot and shunter Class 08 No. 08613 is stabled on the left awaiting its next turn of duty.

John Hillmer

Valley

Crossing the Stanley Embankment, which connects Anglesey with Holy Island, Class 47 No. 47561 hauls the 13.10 Holyhead to Euston on 7th July 1985. In the background can be seen the Anglesey Aluminium smelting plant and the outline of Holyhead Mountain. The water on the left is known as the "Inland Sea".

John Hillmer

◁
Looking something of an anachronism in the late 1980s, the four-wagon Holyhead-Llandudno Junction 'trip' freight ('target 92') passes alongside the Anglesey Aluminium plant near Holyhead on 8th April 1988. Motive power is provided by Class 47 No. 47285, painted in the original Railfreight livery. The train will call at the sidings here to attach a ferry van loaded with aluminium billets, before continuing its journey to Bangor and Llandudno Junction. In addition to the ferry van traffic, there is a weekly trainload of petroleum coke from Immingham to the Anglesey Aluminium plant.

Paul Shannon

◁
Heading the 07.51 York to Holyhead on 7th July 1985, 'Peak' Class 45 No. 45117 comes to a halt in order for the driver to take instructions from the signalman at Valley box. Being a Sunday, maintenance work was being carried out between Valley and Holyhead. Valley station was closed in 1966 but was re-opened in March 1982.

John Hillmer

The 06.20 Holyhead-Stratford Freightliner working, reporting number 4E86, re-starts from a signal check at Valley on 8th April 1988, headed by Class 47 No. 47352.

Paul Shannon

Class 47 No. 47474 accelerates away from Valley with the 16.20 Holyhead-London Euston express on 17th April 1985. Running horizontally across the field on the right is the short branch to Valley Goods, now used almost exclusively for nuclear flask traffic to and from Wylfa Power Station.

Paul Shannon

With its glaring headlight betraying the poor lighting conditions, Class 47 No. 47334 approaches Gaerwen with a trainload of sulphur for Amlwch on 11th August 1987. The train will need to set back over Gaerwen's crossover in order to join the Amlwch branch, since there is no longer a direct connection here from the 'down' line.

Paul Shannon

Class 40 No. 40013 approaches Llanfair P.G. on 12th August 1984, with 1M71, the 07.55 York to Holyhead. In the background, above the locomotive cab, can be seen the Marquis of Anglesey's Column, which, from the top, affords wonderful views of Snowdonia and the Isle of Anglesey.
John Hillmer

On the bright sunny morning of 9th August 1985, a Class 101 three-car unit approaches Gaerwen signal box with a Holyhead to Chester service. The freight only branch to Amlwch leaves the main line at Gaerwen. Note the mast on the cabin for communication with Amlwch when a train is on the branch.
John Hillmer

Class 47 No. 47334 nears its journey's end with the 05.50 Llandudno Junction–Amlwch company train (7D04) on 11th August 1987, conveying seven empty ethylene dibromide tanks and five loaded chlorine tanks from Ellesmere Port. Next to the locomotive are a brake van and ex-VDA barrier vehicle, and this arrangement is repeated at the tail end of the train. The stretch of railway illustrated here leads ¾ mile beyond the original passenger terminus at Amlwch and was constructed as a privately owned light railway in 1952.

Paul Shannon

The 17-mile Amlwch branch has survived as a 'freight only' line for nearly a quarter of a century since the withdrawal of passenger services in December 1964. It is thanks to Associated Octel that the line has been kept relatively busy during this period, with a daily chemicals train to and from Ellesmere Port and occasional consignments of sulphur from Mostyn Dock. On 18th April 1985, Class 47 No. 47128 is seen approaching Llanerchymedd, six miles south of Amlwch, with the 08.25 train from Amlwch to Llandudno Junction and, ultimately, Ellesmere Port.

Paul Shannon

After many years of neglect, the entrepreneurs of the 1980s have seen fit to exploit the tourist potential of Llanfair P.G. and have erected a new collection of shops adjacent to the re-opened station. The extensive car and coach park was occupied only by the photographer's Volkswagen on the morning of 7th April 1988, when Class 150/1 'Sprinter' unit No. 150115 was recorded arriving on the 07.30 Holyhead–Llandudno service.

Paul Shannon

Llanfairpwllgwyngyllgogerychwyrndrobwllllantysiliogogogoch

No book covering North Wales would be complete without a photograph of the full station name which, translated into English, means "St Mary's Church in the hollow of the white hazel near to the rapid whirlpool of St Tysilio's Church by the red cave". Welsh is undoubtedly more economical in the use of letters than English!

John Hillmer

The 15.17 Holyhead–Llandudno 'local' has just left Llanfair P.G. on 17th April 1985, formed by Class 101 cars Nos M51199 and M54334. The signal box at this location remains in use as a crossing keeper's cabin.

Paul Shannon

North Wales Coast – Bangor to Llandudno Junction

Bangor station from the east – Class 45/1 'Peak' No. 45115 stands in the 'up' platform line waiting to depart with the 11.15 service to Newcastle on 18th April 1985. Workmen on the right are recovering sleepers from the former 'up' bay line.
Paul Shannon

Class 25s remained a common sight in North Wales until their final withdrawal from BR service. On 18th April 1985, No. 25229 is pictured setting back on to the 'down' line at Bangor in order to reach the goods yard. The train is 'target 92', on its return leg from Holyhead to Llandudno Junction. The two ferry vans had been collected from the Anglesey Aluminium plant, and these would soon be joined on 'target 92' by two empty cement tanks from Bangor.
Paul Shannon

Bangor's railway facilities are concentrated on a short section of open track between two tunnels – Bangor Tunnel to the east and Belmont Tunnel to the west. Rising above each tunnel mouth are hillsides affording fine views of the station and goods yard. This photograph is taken from above Belmont Tunnel and shows the Class 47-hauled 13.20 Crewe-Holyhead train pulling out of the 'down' platform loop on 16th April 1985. The goods yard, still in regular use for cement traffic in 1988, lies to the right of the field of view.
Paul Shannon

PLAZA
Bangor

ABER

The Kingston Minerals (Granite) sidings at Penmaenmawr generate considerable rail traffic, despatching trains weekdays to Bamber Bridge, Carnforth and other destinations as required. On 26th February 1985, Class 47 No. 47326 shunts in the yard, which contains a large number of departmental ballast wagons plus a rake of HKVs (to the right of the locomotive). The yard has been remodelled to accommodate part of the new A55 road, as seen in the other picture taken on 16th June 1988, with a reduction in the number of sidings. Although now mainly Class 47 hauled, over the years, 40s, 45s, occasional single 20s and 31s have all been employed on stone trains. For almost two years from March 1987 there was a regular FO 2 x 37 turn to Salford Hope Street, formed of 21 bogie hoppers, perhaps the heaviest train ever to run in North Wales.

John Hillmer

On the wintry morning of 13th February 1985, Class 47/4 No. 47612 *Titan* speeds through Llanfairfechan station with the 08.47 Holyhead to Newcastle. Work began in October 1987 on the demolition of the old station and the following year a simpler, but tasteful, new station was opened, the alterations being necessitated by the up-grading of the nearby A55 road.

John Hillmer

◁

Due for abolition in May 1989, Aber box was the only intermediate signal cabin between Bangor and Penmaenmawr. There was a station here until 1960. Class 47 No. 47538 is in charge of the 07.05 Holyhead to Cardiff, on 9th August 1985. For a period Class 33s from the Southern Region worked these trains. From the start of the 1988 summer timetable these services went over to 'Sprinter' operation, routed via Chester and Wrexham, although due to the shortage of units, well into 1989, the 15.00 Cardiff to Rhyl (via Crewe) and return service was often worked by a Class 37/4 from Canton Depot.

John Hillmer

On 2nd May 1985, Class 47 No. 47333 heads the 12.46 Holyhead to Euston through Penmaenmawr station and passes sister locomotive No. 47204 which is waiting to leave the stone sidings with a rake of loaded ballast wagons.
John Hillmer

Class 47 No. 47535 *University of Leicester* approaches Penmaenmawr with the four-coach 17.34 Crewe-Holyhead working of 15th April 1985. The road on the right is the infamous A55, now expanded to dual carriageway proportions at this location.
Paul Shannon

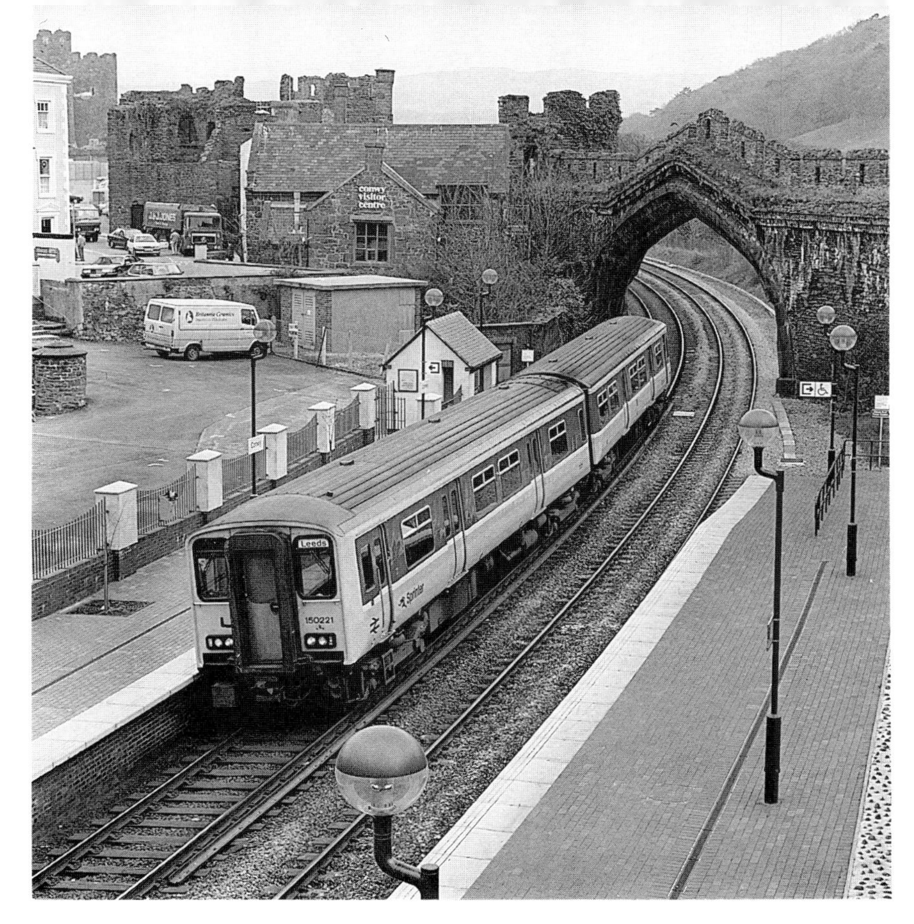

Class 150/2 'Sprinter' unit No. 150221 calls at Conwy on 7th April 1988, forming the 15.20 Holyhead-Hull "Trans-Pennine" service.

Paul Shannon

Conwy's new station was opened on 27th June 1988, on the site of the original station which closed in 1966. The rebuilding costs of £267,000 were shared between Gwynedd County Council and the Welsh Office. Illustrated here on 7th April 1988 is Class 150/1 'Sprinter' unit No. 150135 arriving on the 15.55 Llandudno-Holyhead service, whilst passengers on the 'up' platform await the next eastbound train. It is encouraging to see stations such as this being reopened after many years of dereliction, but equally sad to hear of vandalism occurring to the new facilities provided.

Paul Shannon

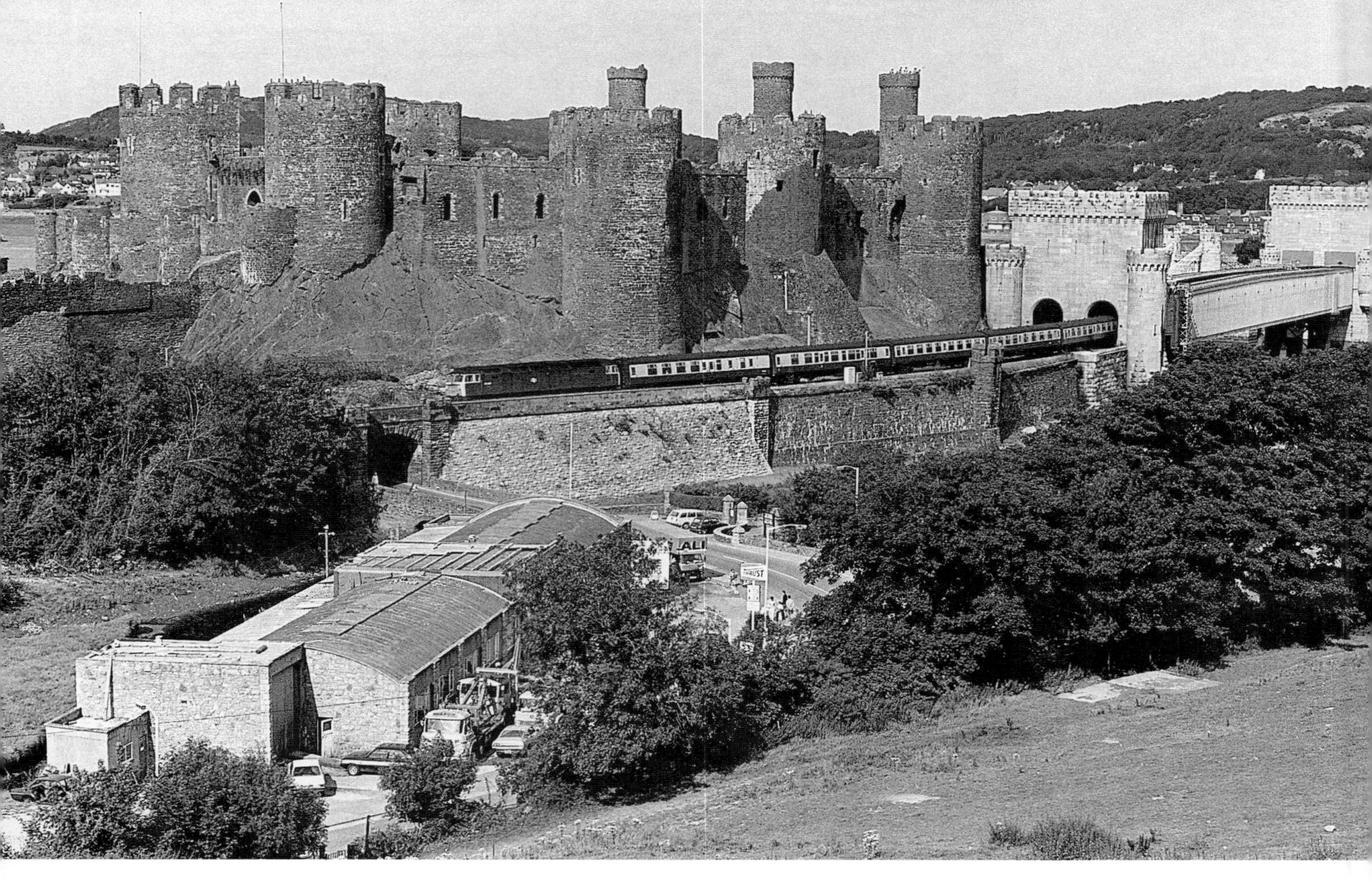

The 13.45 Manchester Victoria to Bangor working skirts Conwy Castle after crossing the estuary on 14th August 1982, formed by Class 47 No. 47437 and a rake of Mk I coaching stock.

Paul Shannon

It is ironic that the new A55 "Expressway" has brought revenue to BR albeit of a temporary nature. New sidings were laid at Conwy Morfa, approximately at the site of the old Military Sidings, west of Conwy, to facilitate the bringing in of building materials for the new road. Class 47 No. 47338 shunts the sidings on 16th June 1988, and will take the two PCA cement wagons to Llandudno Junction yard, where they will form part of the afternoon "Speedlink" to Warrington (Walton Old Junction). A new road tunnel entrance can be seen on the left of the picture.

John Hillmer

Llandudno Junction's freight yard is connected to the main line only at the west end of the station, and all 'up' departures must reverse out of the sidings before commencing their journey. Class 31 No. 31289 is performing this manoeuvre with 7F10, the 15.38 Speedlink service to Warrington, on 10th August 1987. The load on this occasion comprises one ferry van with aluminium billets from Holyhead, two empty PCA cement tanks from Bangor, and one empty HEA hopper from Llandudno Junction coal depot.
Paul Shannon

In the mid-1980s 'Peaks' made a welcome change from the ubiquitous Class 47s on North Wales Coast passenger workings. No. 45125 is seen here approaching Llandudno Junction station with the 11.00 Scarborough-Bangor train of 15th April 1985. The single track on the right leads to Llandudno Junction freight terminal, opened in 1981 to replace facilities displaced elsewhere by the A55 road works.
Paul Shannon

Looking west towards Llandudno Junction station, 'Peak' Class 45 No. 45123 departs with the 08.47 Holyhead to Newcastle on 6th April 1985. These locomotives worked regularly on "Trans-Pennine" trains right up to the winter timetable of 1986/7, although by then they were down to two daily rostered turns in North Wales. They continued to appear spasmodically on passenger workings after this, but by the second half of 1987 were confined to occasional visits to Penmaenmawr on stone trains, although even up to June 1988 there were still odd appearances and No. 45107 worked into Llandudno with an excursion from Chesterfield on the 12th of that month.

John Hillmer

On Saturday morning, 2nd July 1983, Class 40 No. 40047 is at the head of a rake of engineers' wagons. The yard at Llandudno Junction contains a variety of wagons, ranging from modern air-braked PCAs (immediately to the right of the locomotive) to old-fashioned MCV coal trucks (further back in the same rake). This was a transition period for Railfreight, when vacuum and air-braked wagons were both in common use and many trains were formed of a mixture of the two, necessitating the use of a brake van.

John Hillmer

◁

Class 47 No. 47381 stands on the right, with a sister locomotive in the depot at Llandudno Junction, together with a Class 08 shunter on 13th July 1984. By 1988 there were no locomotives or units officially allocated anywhere in North or Mid Wales, even the Holyhead Class 08s being supplied from Crewe T.M.D.

John Hillmer

▷

In order to gain access to the Conwy Valley line, Metropolitan-Cammell Class 101 diesel multiple unit with No. M53222 leading, crosses the main line on 2nd May 1985, with the 14.53 Llandudno to Blaenau Ffestiniog. 'Sprinters' were used on the branch for a time but during 1987 were banned due to excessive noise levels.

John Hillmer

Llandudno & The Conwy Valley

'Sprinter' No. 150150 leaves Llandudno station with the 15.30 to Crewe on 16th June 1988. Present at the same time were 'Pacer' No. 142066 and three West Midland Class 116 sets Nos T338, T326 and T339, all based at Tyseley. The only loco-hauled trains using the station in Summer 1988 were the SO and Sunday single service to Euston, 1A41.

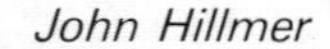

John Hillmer

Llandudno's LNWR design signal box survives to control a number of semaphore signals and turnouts in the station area, despite some rationalisation of the layout in recent years. On 16th April 1985, Class 101 cars Nos M51186 and M54357 are seen shortly after departure on the 17.20 service to Holyhead.

Paul Shannon

On 20th July 1985, Class 47/4 No. 47602 (subsequently to be named *Glorious Devon*) backs into Llandudno station to head 1A41, the 09.39 to Euston. At the time, on Saturdays, there were loco-hauled trains to Euston, Birmingham, Newcastle, York and Stoke-on-Trent.

John Hillmer

Just outside Llandudno station, an unidentified Class 47, in Railfreight livery, waits for departing 15.56 dmu service to Holyhead, on 16th June 1988. The rake of empty HJV wagons, which show signs of having recently been used for carrying raw sulphur from Mostyn Dock, are likely going to be stored for a period near the station.

John Hillmer

BLAENAU FFESTINIOG

Passengers
must not cross
the line

◁

Metropolitan-Cammell Class 101 with No. M53222 leading, leaves Deganwy station with the 14.53 Llandudno to Blaenau Ffestiniog service on 2nd May 1985. To the right lies the River Conwy estuary, currently the scene of great activity, with preparations for the new A55 "Expressway" which will go under the estuary from a point between Deganwy and Llandudno Junction.

John Hillmer

▷

Deganwy is the only intermediate station on the Llandudno branch. In this view a call has just been made there by Class 101 dmu Nos M53328 and M53318, operating the 07.00 service from Blaenau Ffestiniog to Llandudno on 19th April 1985.

Paul Shannon

South of Llandudno Junction, the Blaenau branch runs alongside the Conwy estuary for several miles. Class 47 No. 47352 is pictured near Tal-y-Cafn with 'target 90' trip freight from Maentwrog Road to Llandudno Junction on 7th April 1988. The VAA van is loaded with commercial explosives from Maentwrog to Snodgrass, and will continue its journey on the following day's Llandudno Junction-Warrington Speedlink service. Maentwrog Read was the loading point for the ICI factory at Penrhyndeudraeth on the Cambrian Coast line.

Paul Shannon

Llanrwst is the only crossing place between Llandudno Junction and Blaenau Ffestiniog. Pictured here on 18th April 1985 is Metropolitan-Cammell dmu set Nos M53318 and M53328, forming the 14.53 service from Llandudno. This station was renamed Llanrwst North in 1989 upon the opening of a new station nearer the town centre.

Paul Shannon

Class 101 dmu cars Nos M53318 and M53328 call at Betws-y-Coed station whilst working the 11.05 Llandudno-Blaenau Ffestiniog service on 17th April 1985. This is the most substantial station on the branch, although like the others it is unstaffed. On the right is a rival tourist attraction, the Conwy Valley Railway Museum!

Paul Shannon

Class 47 No. 47352 arrives at Llanrwst with 'target 90' trip freight from Maentwrog Road on 7th April 1988. A short wait will be required here in order for the next southbound passenger working to pass.

Paul Shannon

Class 47 No. 47163 runs round at Blaenau Ffestiniog on 9th August 1985, after arriving with the 11.10 from Llandudno, in readiness for the return working. On the left is the narrow gauge Ffestiniog Railway terminus platform with a train waiting departure to Porthmadog.

John Hillmer

Class 25 No. 25058 has just run round its train of one flask wagon plus barrier vehicles and brake van in the former coal yard at Blaenau Ffestiniog (LNWR) station. As soon as the single line has been cleared by the next passenger service, No. 25058 will propel its train through Blaenau Ffestiniog's new station and then down the branch to Trawsfynydd. The photograph is dated 17th April 1985.

Paul Shannon

The railway to Trawsfynydd winds its way between rows of stone cottages on the south side of Blaenau Ffestiniog before opening out on to bleak and windswept moorland. Class 25 No. 25058 is seen propelling 'target 91' trip freight down the branch line on 17th April 1985, conveying a discharged nuclear flask from Sellafield to Trawsfynydd. Southbound trains always have to be propelled south of Blaenau because there are no rounding facilities at either Trawsfyndd or Maentwrog Road. Passenger services returned to Maentwrog Road in Summer 1989, a new platform having been built north of the old station to accommodate the Sundays only dmu operated service.
Paul Shannon

▽

First generation dmus returned to the Conwy Valley line in 1987 because of excessive noise from the wheel flanges of 'Sprinter' units on the branch. A three-car Class 101 formation, Nos 53331, 59125 and 53308, has just arrived at Blaenau Ffestiniog after working the 09.19 service from Crewe on 10th August 1987. On the left, the tail end of a Ffestiniog Railway train to Porthmadog is just visible.
Paul Shannon

◁

Roman Bridge is the first station out of Blaenau Ffestiniog on the Conwy Valley line to Llandudno Junction. In this beautiful countryside an unidentified Class 25 trundles through with a nuclear flask train on 9th August 1985, from Trawsfynydd Power Station en route to Sellafield in Cumbria.
John Hillmer

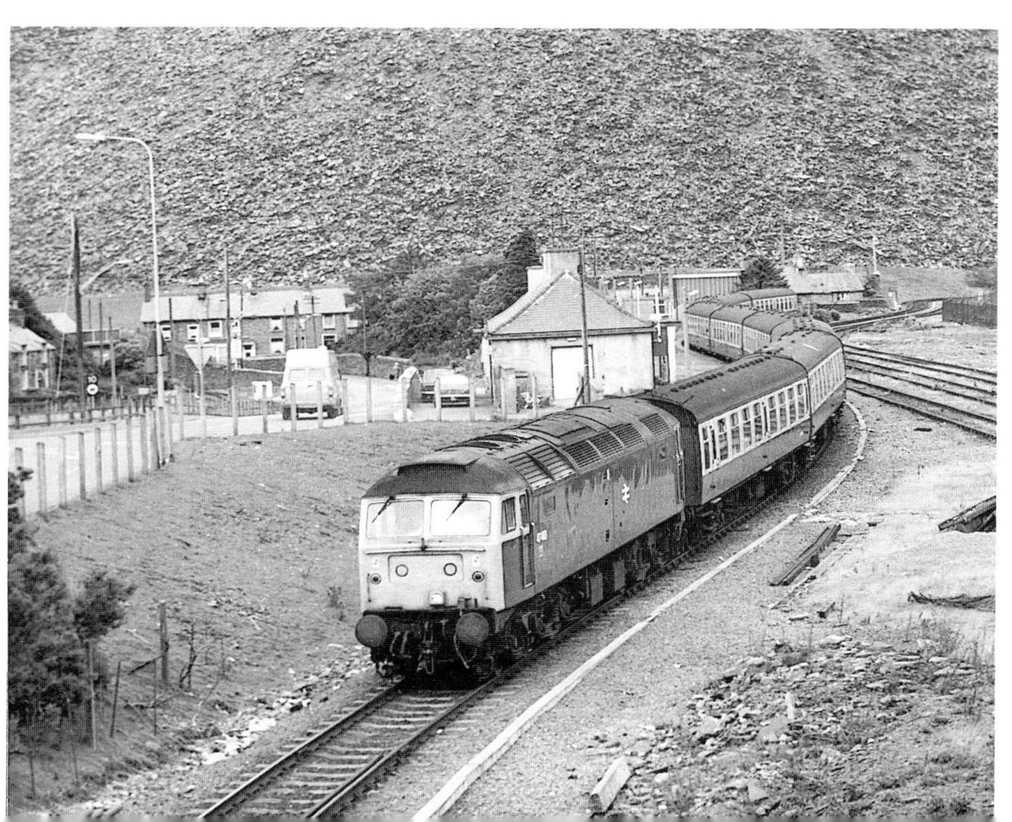

On 9th August 1985, Class 47 No. 47163 passes the old station at Blaenau Ffestiniog with the 11.10 from Llandudno. These loco-hauled trains ran during the summer period, Monday to Friday, but ceased after 1986.
John Hillmer

North Wales Coast – *Llandudno Junction to Chester*

Shortly after leaving Llandudno Junction yard, Class 25 No. 25229 heads east along the main line with 7F10, the 15.38 Llandudno Junction-Warrington Speedlink service, on 18th April 1985. The train is conveying aluminium billets from Holyhead (first and fourth wagons), explosives from Blaenau Ffestiniog, and empty cement tanks from Bangor.
Paul Shannon

With the A55 "Expressway" still under construction, Class 45/0 'Peak' No. 45060 passes Mochdre with the 14.40 Birmingham Lawley Street-Holyhead Freightliner working (4D58) on 16th April 1985. For several years the two 'down' evening Freightliners along the North Wales Coast could be distinguished fairly reliably by their motive power – 'Peaks' on the Lawley Street working, and Class 47s on the train from Trafford Park.
Paul Shannon

Once a four-track stretch, even the reduced double-track railway at Mochdre was moved to allow the construction of the up-graded A55. 'Sprinters', Class 150/2 No. 150208 and Class 150/1 No. 150114 are in multiple forming the 10.02 Bangor to Hull on 25th February 1988.

John Hillmer

Crossing the Tan-y-lan bridge over the A55 "Expressway", Class 47 No. 47521 heads the 11.00 Scarborough to Bangor on 2nd May 1985. In the background can be seen the ornate entrance to Penmaenrhos Tunnel, which pierces the headland, with its crenellated twin towers.

John Hillmer

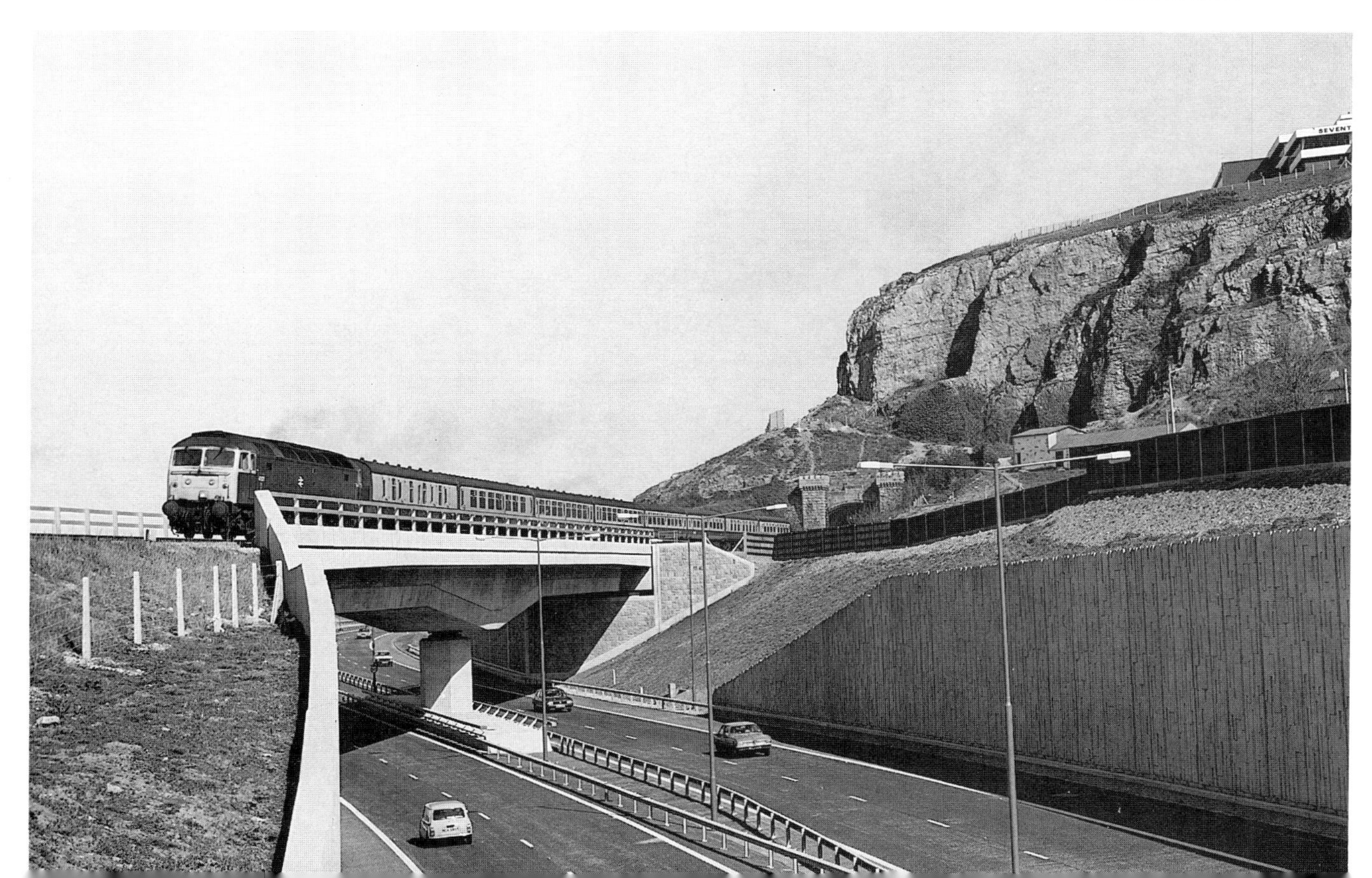

On the beautifully clear morning of 14th August 1982, the 07.55 Llandudno-Crewe diesel multiple unit service hugs the coastline to the east of Colwyn Bay, before diving under the next headland through Penmaenrhos Tunnel. The effect of A55 construction work on this stretch of the coastline is only too evident from this photograph.

Paul Shannon

Class 47 No. 47104 pulls away from Colwyn Bay with the 15.45 Manchester Victoria-Bangor service of 13th August 1982. The siding on the right once led into Colwyn Bay goods yard, now replaced by the facilities at Llandudno Junction.

Paul Shannon

'aken from the road bridge looking east, his view of Abergele & Pensarn station hows a six-car Class 101 set forming the 1.55 (SO) Llandudno to Manchester 'ictoria on 6th April 1985, waiting "for the oad". Subsequently both loops have been emoved and the fast tracks slewed into he platforms, allowing trains to stop if the ignal box is switched out.

John Hillmer

'ramed by Abergele's two bracket signals or 'up' trains, Class 40 No. 40015 is ignalled for the 'down' platform line as it rrives with the 17.27 Crewe-Holyhead vorking of 17th August 1982.

Paul Shannon

:lass 25 No. 25202 speeds through \bergele with 7F10, the 15.38 Llandudno Junction-Warrington Speedlink feeder ervice, on 15th April 1985.

Paul Shannon

With the "peg off" for the through road Class 47 No. 47488 approaches Abergele & Pensarn with the 13.20 Crewe to Holyhead service on 11th March 1985. The signal on the right is for the platform road.
John Hillmer

Looking towards Snowdonia, the hills form a delightful backcloth for Class 47 No. 47485 as it drifts past Rhyl Marine Lake with an early morning Freightliner from Holyhead, on 6th June 1988.

John Hillmer

Class 40 No. 40197 prepares to leave Abergele on 14th August 1982 with the 09.00 Llandudno to York holiday train. Observe the unusual siting of Abergele's signal box, between the 'up' and 'down' through lines.

Paul Shannon

Passing the impressive LNWR Rhyl No. 2 signal box, Class 47 No. 47529 enters the station with the six coach 08.15 Holyhead to Crewe on 27th October 1984. The short signal arms were an unusual feature of Rhyl. Considerable rationalisation has taken place here with the yard having gone completely and there are now only two sidings on the 'down' side, east of the station.

John Hillmer

A pair of Class 25 locomotives, Nos 25153 and 25221, are seen departing from Rhyl station with a summer Saturday holiday train, the 09.00 York/08.57 Sheffield-Llandudno, on 14th August 1982. Presumably the throb of the 25s is being enjoyed by the various heads peering out of carriage windows!

Paul Shannon

Class 40 No. 40015 passes under the finest surviving signal gantry in North Wales (and perhaps in a much wider area) as it leaves Rhyl with the 09.20 Llandudno-Crewe service on 14th August 1982.

Paul Shannon

Class 47 No. 47536 approaches Prestatyn on 19th April 1985, heading the 10.10 Holyhead-London Euston express.

Paul Shannon

Prestatyn station is unusual in so much that there are two 'down' tracks and only one 'up'. In practice it is operated as an island platform station, the one on the left not normally being used. A Class 47 is in charge of the 09.30 Crewe to Holyhead on 27th October 1984.

John Hillmer

During the interesting period when Class 33s worked into North Wales from South Wales, No. 33001 approaches Gronant Crossing with the 14.17 Bangor to Cardiff on 10th September 1985. Whilst the major alterations to Crewe station were being carried out, these trains ran via Wrexham (a more direct route) necessitating the locomotive running round at Chester, but reverted to the Crewe route when the latter station was re-opened. From May 1988 services between Cardiff and North Wales were rostered for 'Sprinter' operation but due to shortage of these units, Class 37s hauling three or four coaches continued to appear well into 1989 as substitutes.

John Hillmer

The 06.55 Point of Ayr Colliery to Fiddlers Ferry Power Station mgr, 7F62, hauled by Class 20s Nos 20007 and 20053, accelerates through Ffynnongroyw on 13th June 1988. Point of Ayr Colliery, seen in the background, is the last working pit in North Wales. On the right is the Dee Estuary, which opens out into the sea beyond the spit of land on which the colliery lies.

John Hillmer

Winter sunlight catches Class 45 'Peak' No. 45144 *Royal Signals*, as it passes Mostyn Dock hauling 1E99, the 11.15 Bangor to Newcastle on 26th November 1984. The remains of the original station building, designed by Francis Thompson, and opened in 1848, can be seen on the left. The station closed in 1966. On the skyline, on the Welsh side of the Dee Estuary, is Point of Ayr Colliery.

John Hillmer

MOSTYN

A Penmaenmawr to Tue Brook (Liverpool) ballast train, with Class 47 No. 47453 in charge, passes the site of the old station at Holywell Junction (closed in 1966) on 26th June 1988. The station building is another fine example of the work of Francis Thompson. The sidings are used at times for storing mgr wagons for use at Point of Ayr Colliery.

John Hillmer

◁
The sidings in the previous picture held wagons containing raw sulphur, which was unloaded from ships at Mostyn Dock and then moved by rail to Associated Octel at Amlwch. On 18th February 1987, privately owned 0-4-0 diesel electric shunter No. 1 (Yorkshire 2627 of 1956) is marshalling HKV and HJV wagons. In 1988 the main sidings were also used for the movement of steel for construction work in the up-grading of the A55 road.

John Hillmer

◁
A three-car Class 120 diesel multiple unit forming the 07.06 Bangor to Manchester Victoria, passes Mostyn signal box on 2nd July 1985. The cabin was normally open in the morning only, when freight traffic was ready for despatch or when empty wagons were received. These trains only ran "as required" and were thus difficult to photograph!

John Hillmer

On New Year's Eve 1985, a Class 47 heads the 11.00 Euston to Holyhead train along the straight stretch of track at Glan-y- don, between Greenfield and Mostyn. The ex-Heysham to Belfast Ferry, *Duke of Lancaster*, seen in the background, is permanently moored and used as an entertainment centre.

John Hillmer

◄

.ooking north from Greenfield, one of the hree morning Freightliners from Holyhead, ieaded by Class 47 No. 47345, passes the ıld Courtaulds textile factory, on 13th June 988. There is a long siding on the left vhich runs through to Holywell Junction ınd the overgrown one on the right was ısed for the nearby works, but is no longer n use. Prior to the closure of the Courtaulds factory there was a weekly oil rain from Milford Haven but this had eased to run by July 1985.

John Hillmer

►

Rounding the "S" curve from the Greenfield direction, Class 45, No. 45134 ıears Bagillt with the "Trans-Pennine" 15.10 Bangor to Scarborough on 11th March 1985. Across the flat ground to the ight lies the River Dee Estuary, which separates Wales from the Wirral Peninsula n England.

John Hillmer

Through the lattice of a footbridge, Class 40 No. 40167 approaches Flint on 1st August 1981 with the 14.00 Llandudno to York. For so long, Class 40s were the mainstay of services on the North Wales Coast main line, and even the last few locomotives of the class, transferred to Departmental Stock, continued to work to Penmaenmawr, on stone trains, prior to withdrawal.

John Hillmer

Apart from the Euston services, during Summer 1988 the only other regular loco-hauled passenger train on the North Wales Coast was the 07.31 Hull to Holyhead and 13.22 return working. On the wet afternoon of 13th August 1988, Class 31 No. 31463 passes the small tidal pool at Bagillt, with the east-bound train.

John Hillmer

ROCKCLIFFE HALL

The platform-mounted signal box at Flint is another which was only in use "as required", and abolished during 1989. In this picture, Class 45 No. 45122 stops with the 11.15 Bangor to Newcastle on 26th January 1985.

John Hillmer

Class 25 No. 25316 passes Rockcliffe Hall, between Shotton and Flint, with a 'down' empty ballast train for Penmaenmawr on 15th April 1985. On the left, behind the signal box, are the disused Connah's Quay Power Station sidings.

Paul Shannon

An interesting feature of the coast line is its use by the "Test Train" from Crewe, giving trials to locomotives just "shopped" from the Works. The coaches used have been withdrawn from normal service and the windows are boarded up. Here, Class 37/4 No. 37416 (ex-37302) is seen returning to Crewe from Llandudno on 22nd August 1985.

John Hillmer

Storm clouds gather overhead as Class 47 No. 47510 approaches Shotton with the 17.07 Holyhead-Crewe service of 12th August 1982. No. 47510 has since been fitted with push-pull equipment for use by ScotRail, renumbered 47713, and named *Tayside Region.*

Paul Shannon

As an alternative to using the Crewe "Test Train" for running-in ex-works locomotives, they act as "pilots" on normal service trains, so double-heading is a regular feature of the coast line in North Wales. Class 47 No. 47443 leads No. 47459 on the 09.30 Euston to Holyhead on 18th February 1987. Ex-works Class 56s have also appeared on these turns with Class 47s. A 'Pacer' can be seen in the background crossing the main line, with a Wrexham Central to Bidston service.

John Hillmer

A piece of good fortune enabled the photographer to catch Class 45 No. 45126 with a 'down' ballast train going under the Wrexham Central to Bidston line, as Class 37s Nos 37174 and 37222 approach Dee Marsh Junction with steel coil from South Wales on 18th February 1987. The High and Low Level stations at Shotton are connected by a footpath, with the ticket office etc. on the upper level 'down' platform.

John Hillmer

◁

Class 45 No. 45107 passed the imposing cooling towers of the closed Connah's Quay Power Station, on 6th April 1985, with the "coast to coast" 13.24 Llandudno to Scarborough service.

John Hillmer

SANDYCROFT

◁

The winter sun casts long shadows across the four tracks at Sandycroft on 19th December 1986, as 'Peak' Class 45 No. 45103 passes the box with the 10.44 Holyhead to Newcastle service. Class 47 No. 47281, with an engineer's train, stands in the 'down' loop from Mold Junction (which was subsequently abolished in September 1987).

John Hillmer

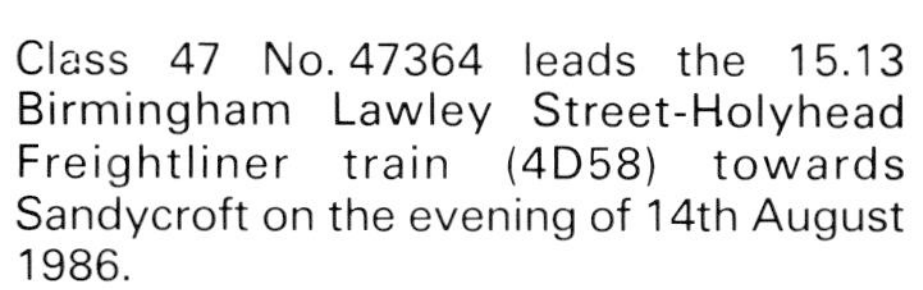

Class 47 No. 47364 leads the 15.13 Birmingham Lawley Street-Holyhead Freightliner train (4D58) towards Sandycroft on the evening of 14th August 1986.

Paul Shannon

Class 25 No. 25058 runs through the flat countryside between Sandycroft and Mold Junction on 24th April 1985, with the afternoon "Speedlink" from Llandudno Junction to Warrington (Walton Old Junction). The formation is: two IPA (aluminium from Holyhead), one TTA (empty to Stanlow), one PCA (empty from Bangor to Penyffordd), one CAR brake van, one RBX barrier van, one FNB nuclear flask wagon, one RBX barrier van, four HEA (empty from Llandudno Junction) and one CAR brake van.

John Hillmer

◁

Approaching Sandycroft from the Chester direction on 24th May 1988, Class 31 No. 31286 trundles through with over 40 ZHV trucks. These locomotives are the natural successors to the Class 25s and are making an increasing number of appearances on the coast line.

John Hillmer

Class 25 No. 25296 prepares to leave the 'up' side sidings at Mold Junction on 20th September 1985 with empty ZHV wagons. The sidings are used for spoil tippings for the Civil Engineer. A Holyhead bound Freightliner is disappearing on the left. The houses to the right of the picture were built for railway workers who would have been employed at the steam shed. The 'down' sidings are not in use. Mold Junction lost its junction status in 1962, when the line to Denbigh was closed, although the nomenclature has remained in use ever since.

John Hillmer

Winter sun catches Class 47/4 No. 47632 passing Mold Junction box on 19th December 1986, with the 11.16 Crewe to Holyhead. No longer a junction, this was once a busy railway centre with extensive freight sidings and a quite modern looking steam shed (coded 6B), the building of which still stands in private industrial use.

John Hillmer

An unusual liveried two-car Class 101 diesel multiple unit passes Roodee Junction, on the western outskirts of Chester, forming the 07.30 Shrewsbury to Chester on 19th June 1985.

John Hillmer

◁

In a snow-covered landscape a Class 101 diesel multiple unit crosses the River Dee with the 15.15 Chester to Shrewsbury service on 11th February 1985. On the right is the Roodee Racecourse with the City of Chester in the background.

John Hillmer

Close to the City wall, Class 25 No. 25321 crosses the Shropshire Union Canal at Chester on 19th June 1985 with a westbound train made up of POA wagons for Shotton Steel Works.

John Hillmer

Looking east towards the City of Chester on 24th April 1985, Class 47 No. 47202 heads for Wales with empty mgr wagons bound for either Bersham (then still producing coal) or Point of Ayr Collieries.
John Hillmer

Class 31/4 No. 31442 passes Chester Depot (CH) on 26th March 1988, with the SO 06.17 Holyhead to Manchester Red Bank empty vans and TPO. On the other days of the week the train ran from Bangor. On this occasion it would call at the yard by Chester station before heading east.
John Hillmer

Sprinter Class 150/2 No. 150202, on the left of the picture, arriving at Chester with the 06.27 from Leeds to Holyhead service. Two other Class 150s can also be seen in the station. The only timetabled loco-hauled passenger trains by Summer 1988 on the North Wales coast line were on the services between Holyhead and Euston and on Saturdays the 07.31 from Hull to Holyhead and return working. Oh for the days of "Whistlers" and 'Peaks' – how they are missed!

John Hillmer

With the imposing Chester No. 2 signal box dominating the scene, Class 47 No. 47192 sets off after a brief stop on the goods lines with 6F25, the 10.42 merry-go-round train from Bersham to Fiddlers Ferry, on 13th August 1982.

Paul Shannon

Deeside to Wrexham

△

The direct line between Mickle Trafford and Dee Marsh Junction was closed for economy's sake on 14th May 1984, but reopened as a single track route on 1st September 1986, thanks to an upturn in steel coil traffic to BSC Shotton. Class 20 locomotives Nos 20009 and 20154 are approaching the site of Sealand station on 17th October 1987 with the 05.25 Mossend–Dee Marsh Junction coil train (6M24). These locomotives would have taken over from electric traction at Warrington Bank Quay. In 1988 there were three daily coil trains over the reopened line, together with return 'empties', and there was also an evening Speedlink service from Warrington to Dee Marsh Junction and back. In early 1989 the steel coil workings were re-diagrammed from pairs of Class 20s to Cardiff-based Class 37/7s.

Paul Shannon

Looking west, across the bridge over the River Dee, 'Pacer' No. 142015 nears Hawarden Bridge station with a Wrexham Central to Bidston service, on 7th May 1988. Virtually all passenger trains are operated by 'Pacers', with occasional appearances by 'Sprinters' and older generation units. This pair is unusual in being painted in chocolate and cream livery, showing that it worked in Devon and Cornwall when new and then having the nickname of "Skippers".

John Hillmer

◁

A two-car Class 101 diesel multiple unit prepares to stop at Hawarden Bridge with the 16.41 from Bidston to Wrexham Central in August 1985. Dee Marsh Junction signal box can be seen in the background, and to the left is the entry to Dee Marsh freight yard, which receives steel coil from BSC plants at Ravenscraig, Llanwern and Port Talbot, for the John Summers Steel Works at Shotton (now part of BSC). Pairs of Class 37s worked these trains from South Wales until May 1987, when single Class 37/9s took over with pairs of Class 20s working to Scotland, via the freight only line to Mickle Trafford. There is also daily Speedlink traffic from Warrington Arpley bringing timber to the Shotton Paper Co. and chemicals to the Deeside Titanium plant.

John Hillmer

◁

iteel coil is received at Shotton from both
icotland and South Wales. The latter flow
i illustrated here on 26th September 1987,
vith Class 37/9 No. 37901 heading north
rom Buckley with the 02.45 working from
ievern Tunnel Junction (6M44). The coil
i positioned over the bogies of the
BA/BAA wagons, in order to minimise the
train on the wagon floors.

Paul Shannon

Class 56 No. 56008 heads north through
Penyffordd on 31st January 1985, with
oaded steel coil BBA wagons from South
Wales to the BSC works at Shotton. These
rains are currently in the hands of single
Class 37/9s. Class 56s were used regularly
on the Birmingham (Curzon Street) to
ement trains and loaded return workings
rom Penyffordd cement works, as well as
pairs of Class 20s and the very rare
ppearance of a Class 58. Otherwise Class
56s in North Wales have been mainly
onfined to the occasional mgr working
nd "running-in" turns from Crewe on the
oast line. The former branch to Mold can
be seen on the left hand side. This was
officially closed on 9th September 1984.

John Hillmer

The lattice type footbridge gives away the GCR/LNER history of the Bidston to Wrexham Central line, which was these companies' only access into Wales. Looking towards Shotton, a Class 108 unit, with No. M51950 leading, stops at Hawarden station on 26th November 1984 with a local service.

John Hillmer

On 25th June 1985, Class 47 No. 47313 approaches Cefn-y- Bedd station with a mixed train of cement wagons from Penyffordd and empty timber wagons from Shotton, forming the daily return Speedlink service from Dee Marsh Junction to Warrington Arpley.

John Hillmer

Once a terminal station, before the extension to Central was built, Wrexham Exchange was reduced to one platform in use when the line was singled to Central. Since this picture was taken of a Class 101 unit on 28th February 1985, forming the 13.25 service from Wrexham Central to Bidston, the name "Exchange" has been dropped and the station is now considered to be part of the adjacent General station, seen on the right. The footbridge at General was to be extended across to the ex-GC line station for easier access.

John Hillmer

▷

A two-car Class 108 diesel multiple unit forms the 15.15 departure from Wrexham Central to Bidston on 11th August 1982. This single bare platform is all that remains of Wrexham Central station.

Paul Shannon

Chester to Shrewsbury

Class 47 No. 47616 approaches Rossett with the 06.25 Chester to Euston train on 8th June 1985. Since then, the loops have been removed, and after considerable local opposition, the line between Chester and Wrexham had been reduced to single track by Easter 1986. This train ceased to run at the end of the winter timetable in May 1986, thus Wrexham lost its only through service to Euston.

John Hillmer

Class 47 No. 47192 approaches Wrexham General with 6J25, the 13.45 merry-go-round 'empties' from Fiddlers Ferry to Bersham on 12th August 1982. At that time there were two signal boxes facing each other across the tracks at this point: one for the ex-GWR route (behind the locomotive) and another for the ex-GCR line to Bidston (on the left). Subsequently the latter has been moved to the Great Central Railway at Loughborough.

Paul Shannon

◁

On the wintry afternoon of 18th February 1985, the 13.15 Chester to Aberystwyth stops at Wrexham General, formed of a six-car Class 108 dmu. Most services on this line are now operated by 'Sprinters'. Although the majority of trains run between Chester and Shrewsbury, Wrexham maintains a through morning service from Holyhead to Cardiff and an afternoon return working.

John Hillmer

Looking south towards Croes Newydd North Fork crossing, HST No. 253045 approaches Wrexham General station, on Sunday 21st August 1988, forming the 09.20 Plymouth to Liverpool Lime Street. This was the first timetabled appearance of an InterCity 125 into North Wales.

John Hillmer

During the period when Crewe station was undergoing major rationalisation, Class 33 No. 33035 enters Wrexham General station with the diverted 14.17 Bangor to Cardiff service on 25th June 1986, necessitating the locomotive running-round at Chester.

John Hillmer

Class 25 No. 25080 poses for the photographer beside Croes Newydd North Fork signal box on 11th April 1982. The tracks leading to the left in the foreground gave access to Croes Newydd marshalling yard and the Brymbo branch.

Paul Shannon

Situated just to the south of Wrexham General station, Croes Newydd North Fork signal box controls the road crossing and Watery Road sidings. On 25th June 1985, a Shrewsbury to Chester diesel multiple unit passes the daily "Speedlink" on its return trip from Dee Marsh to Warrington Arpley. The train has come down the ex-LNER metals via the connection at the north end of General/Exchange stations, from Dee Marsh having called at Penyffordd cement works, and will return north via the ex-GWR line to Chester en route for its destination of Arpley. The Class 47 is "off picture", in the process of running round its train.

John Hillmer

Class 25 No. 25135 sets off from Croes Newydd yard towards Wrexham on the morning of 12th August 1982, with a single GUV parcels van in tow. This was a short trip working from Wrexham General 'up' side to Wrexham General 'down' side via the Croes Newydd triangle, reversing at both Croes Newydd South Fork and Croes Newydd East. The triangle was closed in March 1983, following the cessation of traffic to and from the Brymbo branch in October 1982.

Paul Shannon

Situated between Wrexham and Shrewsbury, Bersham Colliery was the most recent pit to close in North Wales, leaving only Point of Ayr Colliery in operation. On 25th June 1985, a Class 120 unit has just passed Bersham Sidings signal box, which was only used when there were empties arriving or loaded coal wagons ready to leave the mine. Mgrs ran to Ironbridge or Fiddlers Ferry with stockpiled coal at the end of 1986 and into the first few weeks of 1987, after the pit closed. The box ceased operation in February 1987 following closure of the pit and the signal arms were removed.

John Hillmer

A Class 120 dmu with a Class 101 trailer leaves Chirk with the 08.50 Shrewsbury to Chester service on 23rd October 1984. The sidings on the right lead to the Kronospan works where chipboard is manufactured. A new service commenced early in 1989 bringing in timber, mainly from East Anglia, by Speedlink from Warrington for the final part of the journey.

John Hillmer

◁

Just south of Chirk, the River Ceiriog forms the border between England and Wales. A named, but unidentified, Class 47 crosses the viaduct with the 06.25 Chester to Euston on 6th June 1985. Below it, the aqueduct runs parallel to the railway line carrying the Shropshire Union Canal.

John Hillmer

▷

Ruabon is the first station out of Wrexham on the line to Shrewsbury. A two-car Metropolitan–Cammell Class 101 unit, with No. 53312 leading, enters the station on 20th September 1985 with a Shrewsbury to Chester service. The box was subsequently closed in 1987, having been almost permanently switched out for several years prior to this.

John Hillmer

SHREWSBURY
Ruabon

150 108

Railfreight liveried Class 31 No. 31226 awaits the "all clear" at Gobowen South on 22nd August 1985, before setting off down the Blodwell branch with empty ballast hoppers from Bescot. Gobowen South signal box was closed in June 1987, and the Blodwell branch junction is now controlled from a power-operated ground frame, released from Gobowen North box.
Paul Shannon

◁

One location that has survived the recent rationalisation of trackwork and signalling on the Shrewsbury–Chester line is Weston Rhyn, between Gobowen and Chirk. Still boasting a GWR design signal box, lower and upper quadrant semaphores, and loops on both sides of the main line, Weston Rhyn is pictured here on 26th September 1987, as Class 150/1 'Sprinter' unit No. 150108 passes through on the 14.03 Wolverhampton–Chester service.
Paul Shannon

Class 25 No. 25042 passes under the loading apparatus at Blodwell quarry on 21st August 1985, after working 7J02, the 10.12 'empties' from Bescot. The branch saw its last stone train on 28th October 1988 (hauled by a Class 31), but as there is the possibility of further traffic in the future, the track has not been lifted.
Paul Shannon

Class 47 No. 47230 approaches Haughton, between Shrewsbury and Gobowen, with the 07.20 Llanwern–Dee Marsh Junction steel coil train (6M33) on 19th April 1985.
Paul Shannon

Shrewsbury Coton Hill yard remains open in 1990 as the destination of a daily Speedlink service from Bescot and as the base for local trip workings in the Shrewsbury area. Pictured leaving the yard on 13th August 1987 is Class 37 No. 37235 with 7G19, the 13.39 return Speedlink service to Bescot. The two petroleum tanks had been discharged at Shrewsbury Abbey oil terminal, which closed in Summer 1988. Running along the left hand side of the yard is the double-track line to Wrexham and Chester.
Paul Shannon

The 15.28 Blodwell–Bescot ballast train, reporting number 7G25, passes Haughton on 19th April 1985 in the charge of Class 25 No. 25209. The signal box and 'up' loop at Haughton are only used when the twice-weekly Stanlow–Whittington oil train requires to run round here; the box is also unusual in being without an electrical power supply.
Paul Shannon

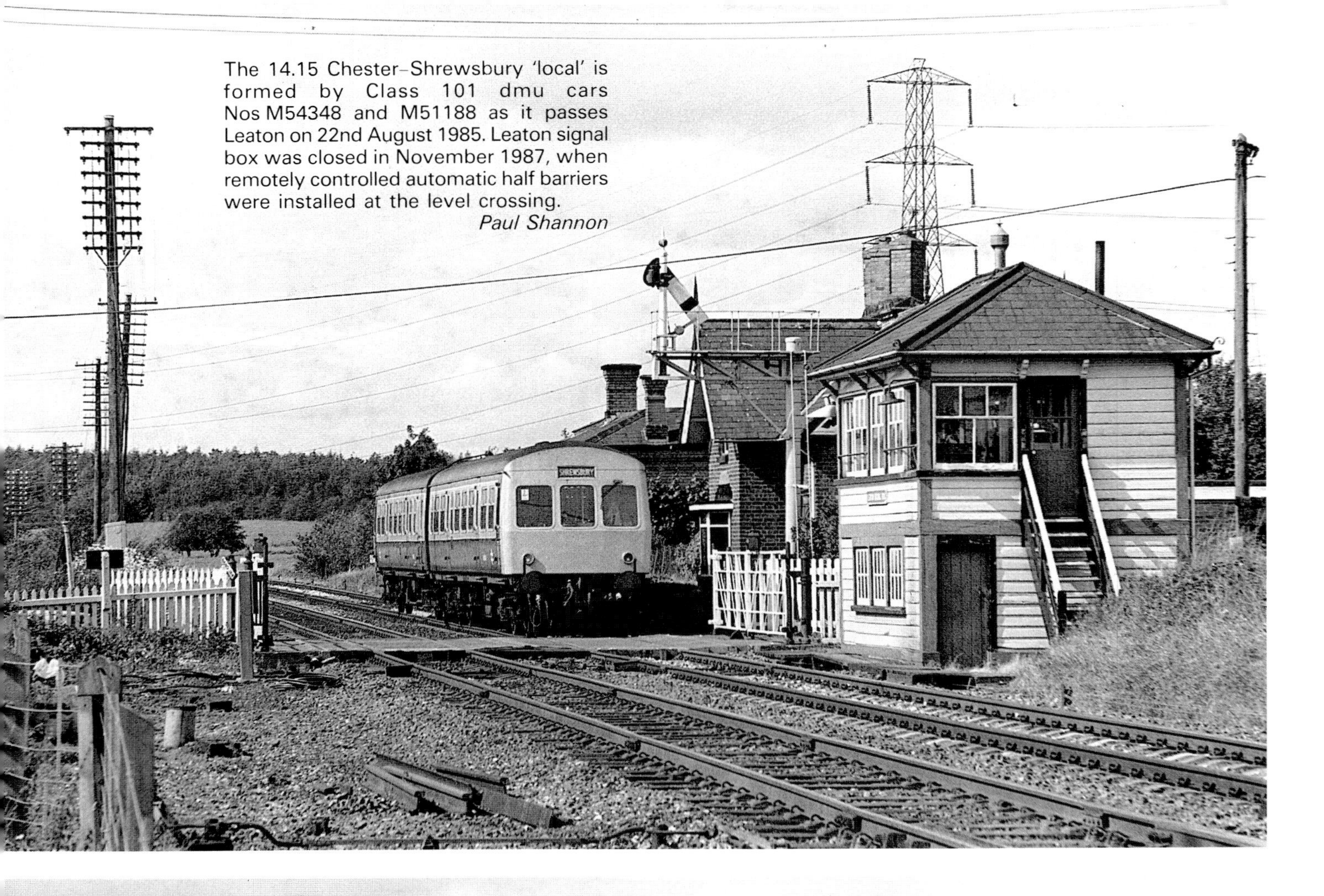

The 14.15 Chester–Shrewsbury 'local' is formed by Class 101 dmu cars Nos M54348 and M51188 as it passes Leaton on 22nd August 1985. Leaton signal box was closed in November 1987, when remotely controlled automatic half barriers were installed at the level crossing.
Paul Shannon

Framed by the lower quadrant signal gantry at the north end of Shrewsbury station is Class 120 'cross-country' unit Nos M50655, M59263 and M50697, forming the 16.15 departure to Crewe on 10th August 1982.
Paul Shannon

◄
:lass 47 No. 47108 approaches
;hrewsbury station on 10th August
982 with 6G29, the 14.46 Penyffordd–
)akengates cement train. In 1988
)akengates received its cement by way of
he thrice-weekly block train to
;irmingham Curzon Street, and the
'acuum-braked Presflo vehicles illustrated
ere had been superseded by air-braked
'CA tanks.

Paul Shannon

Sprinter' No. 150111 arrives in one of the
wo bays at the west end of Shrewsbury
tation, on the sunny winter's morning of
1st December 1987, and will form the
2.41 to Aberystwyth. The first production
Sprinters' for working on the Cambrian
rrived in 1986, although prototype 150001
ommenced trials in October 1985. Other
han the loco-hauled trains, all services
vent over to 'Sprinters' from the
ommencement of the May 1986
imetable.

John Hillmer

Class 37s Nos 37683 and 37682 (borrowed from the Freight Sector) arrive at Shrewsbury on Saturday 21st May 1988 with the 10.10 Aberystwyth to Euston service. The locomotives ran round the train and took it south to Wolverhampton, where they would normally be replaced by an electric locomotive. On the station stabling point sister locomotives Nos 37427 *Bont Y Bermo* and 37429 *Eisteddfod Genedlaethol* are in readiness to take out the 09.40 Euston to Aberystwyth. The fine LNWR signal box is in the fork of the two lines while on the skyline can be seen the Lord Hill Monument, and to the right is the Abbey Church. The platforms at the west end of the station actually span the River Severn.

John Hillmer

Cambrian Main Line

Timber traffic to Welshpool was sadl short-lived. On 21st August 1985, Class 2 No. 25201 approaches Sutton Bridg Junction, Shrewsbury, with the then dail 'target 71' trip working from Coton Hi yard. The train is carrying five OBAs wit timber from Fort William to Welshpoo and two bogie bolster wagons with rail for Hookagate permanent way depot.

Paul Shanno

Scottish timber is being unloaded in th small yard at Welshpool from Railfreigh OBA wagons on 15th June 1985. Thi traffic ceased later that year due to th timber factory running into financia difficulties and the yard has since bee lifted.

John Hillme

About to depart from Welshpool, Class 37 No. 37164 is in charge of the 07.53 Shrewsbury to Aberystwyth on Saturday 15th June 1985. There was considerable local opposition to BR plans to make this an unmanned station. With a new road by-pass approved, BR were to seek parliamentary sanction for line deviation and a new station to serve the town.
John Hillmer

Crossing the River Severn at Caersws, Class 37, No. 37428 *David Lloyd George* heads the 08.00 Pwllheli to Euston ("The Snowdonian") on Saturday 25th June 1988.
John Hillmer

PWLLHELI
60S

37688
688
Great Rocks
37380

The 16.45 Pwllheli-Machynlleth working leaves the remote outpost of Dovey Junction on 12th August 1987, formed by Class 150/1 'Sprinter' units Nos 150134 and 150112. Dovey Junction retained a particularly fine selection of GWR design signalling when this photograph was taken, but the track layout was severely rationalised in May 1988, leaving only a handful of signals controlled by the signal box on the platform.

Paul Shannon

◁

Class 37 No. 37164 brings in the 11.10 Aberystwyth to Euston on 15th June 1985, crossing with a six-car Class 108 dmu forming the 08.43 Birmingham New Street to Pwllheli. Machynlleth station building has been sold and may become a Welsh Museum of Modern Art. A simpler structure will be erected for railway use.

John Hillmer

◁

In the latest two-tone Railfreight livery, Class 37s Nos 37688 *Great Rocks* and 37380 draw forward with 1J18, the 06.20 Birmingham New Street to Aberystwyth at Newtown on 25th June 1988. Most of the Class 37s used on the Cambrian are 37/4s from Cardiff, but on summer Saturdays in 1988 there was one turn allocated to 37/5s based at Tinsley. As the name *Great Rocks* implies, this locomotive is normally employed on stone trains from the Buxton area. The token for single line working will be exchanged at the signal box.

John Hillmer

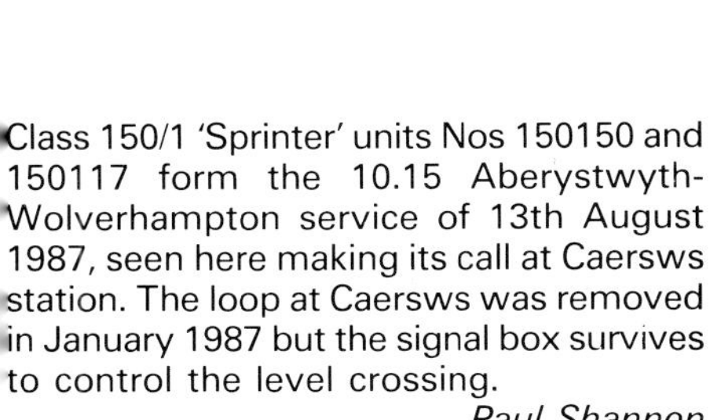

Class 150/1 'Sprinter' units Nos 150150 and 150117 form the 10.15 Aberystwyth-Wolverhampton service of 13th August 1987, seen here making its call at Caersws station. The loop at Caersws was removed in January 1987 but the signal box survives to control the level crossing.

Paul Shannon

'Sprinter' units Nos 150150 and 150132 arrive at Machynlleth on 12th August 1987, forming the 10.50 service from Shrewsbury to Aberystwyth. The driver is about to hand his single line token to the signalman standing on the right. In the shed are a Class 116 dmu from the West Midlands fleet and ex-GWR 'Manor' Class 4-6-0 No. 7819 *Hinton Manor* from the Severn Valley Railway, used during Summer 1987 on the steam specials.

Paul Shannon

The only trains to stop at Dovey Junctio are those providing connections betwee Aberystwyth and the Cambrian Coast lin to Pwllheli. Here, on 12th August 1987 'Sprinter' units Nos 150134 and 150112 ar arriving on the 16.45 Pwllheli-Machynllet service, whilst sister unit No. 150118 wait to continue its journey on the 15.29 servic from Birmingham New Street t Aberystwyth.

Paul Shanno

▷

The sheep seem unperturbed by th passing of the Aberystwyth-Stanlow o 'empties' between Ynyslas and Dove Junction on 6th April 1988. The haulag is Class 20 locomotives Nos 20170 (i Railfreight livery) and 20040, the stoc comprising 13 TTA tank wagons.

Paul Shanno

Approaching Borth on the evening of 5th April 1988 is 'Sprinter' unit No. 150106, forming the 18.20 departure from Aberystwyth to Birmingham New Street. Borth lost is crossing loop and signal box in 1978.
Paul Shannon

On 15th June 1985, Class 37 No. 37167, carrying the "Welsh Lamb" symbol of Cardiff Canton depot, stands at the head of the 13.40 to Shrewsbury by the narrow gauge Vale of Rheidol Railway's shed, the last steam operated service owned by BR but which was subsequently sold to the owners of the Brecon Mountain Railway.
John Hillmer

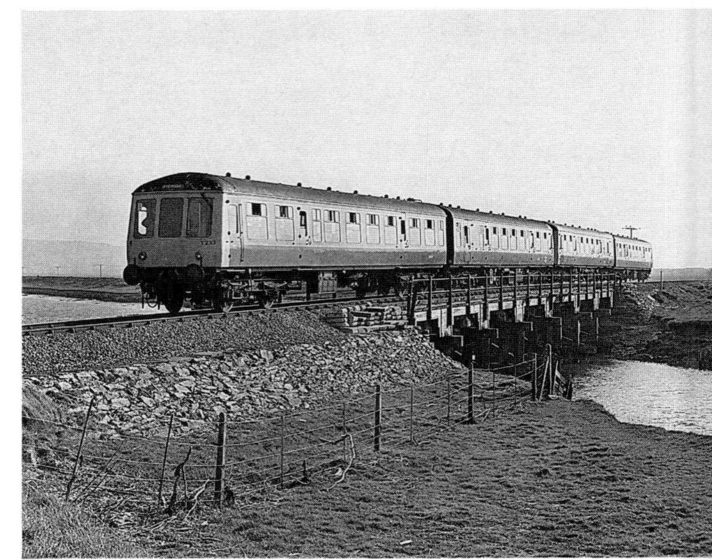

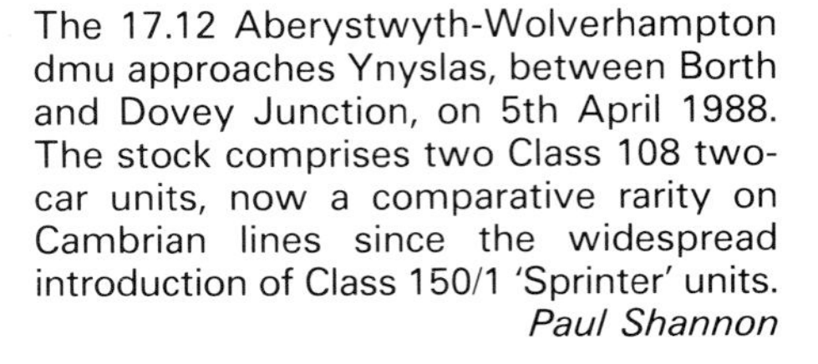

The 17.12 Aberystwyth-Wolverhampton dmu approaches Ynyslas, between Borth and Dovey Junction, on 5th April 1988. The stock comprises two Class 108 two-car units, now a comparative rarity on Cambrian lines since the widespread introduction of Class 150/1 'Sprinter' units.
Paul Shannon

Borth is the only intermediate station between Dovey Junction and Aberystwyth. Class 37 No. 37256 (subsequently reclassified 37/5 and re-numbered 37678) prepares to stop with the 09.35 Euston to Aberystwyth on 15th June 1985.
John Hillmer

The only revenue-earning freight traffic over former Cambrian metals today is the Wednesdays-only oil train from Stanlow to Aberystwyth. This train was the preserve of Class 25 traction for many years, but following the demise of that class pairs of Class 20s became the norm. Nos 20040 and 20170 are pictured arriving at Aberystwyth station on 6th April 1988, having worked 6J28, the 01.00 departure from Stanlow. They must now complete their shunting manoeuvres and 'lock' themselves away from the main running line before the next dmu can be released from Dovey Junction.

Paul Shannon

Class 37s Nos 37182 and 37167 are about to draw forward after having brought in 1J20, the 07.30 from Euston on 15th June 1985. They will run round the stock and take out the return 2J22 to Shrewsbury. It is likely that there will be major re-developments taking place at Aberystwyth station in the future.

John Hillmer

Cambrian Coast

Passing near the site of Abertafol halt between Penhelig and Dovey Junction 'Sprinter' units Nos 150116 and 15013 form the 15.00 service from Pwllheli t Machynlleth. At Machynlleth a connectio will be made with the 17.12 Aberystwyth Wolverhampton service.

Paul Shanno

The 16.37 Machynlleth-Pwllheli servic pulls away from Penhelig halt on 12t August 1987. On the right is the attractiv Dovey Estuary, visible from most of th line between Dovey Junction an Aberdyfi.

Paul Shanno

'ywyn was still fully signalled with lower uadrant semaphores when this hotograph was taken on 13th August 987, showing 'Sprinter' unit No. 150108 rriving on the 13.52 Pwllheli-Machynlleth ervice.

Paul Shannon

ooking south over the road crossing from armouth station, shortly after the arrival rom Machynlleth of Metropolitan-ammell Class 101 two-car unit formed of Jos M53306 and M53325, on 23rd eptember 1985. New barriers were nstalled in 1988. Initially they were nanually controlled but eventually they vould be train-operated, resulting in the losure of Barmouth South signal box. Iowever, the box was a listed building and vas to remain in situ.

John Hillmer

Previous pages:
The glorious view looking north, from the vantage point of Harlech Castle, makes a dramatic background for the 15.30 Pwllheli to Euston, (summer SO) 1A84, hauled by Class 37s Nos 37426 *Y Lein Fach – Vale of Rheidol* and 37429 *Eisteddfod Genedlaethol* on 26th September 1987.

John Hillmer

Token exchange on the Cambrian – a scene soon to disappear with the advent of radio signalling. The 14.10 from Machynlleth is just arriving at Tywyn on 12th August 1987, formed by Class 150/1 unit No. 150112.

Paul Shannon

Barmouth Bridge, over the estuary of the River Mawddach, was closed for a period when the structure was found to be under attack by marine shipworm and considered dangerous. Subsequently re-opened with loco-hauled trains permitted, the summer SO Euston to Pwllheli trains are now in the hands of double-headed Class 37s. In this picture, No. 37426 *Y Lein Fach – Vale of Rheidol* and No. 37429 *Eisteddfod Genedlaethol* across the bridge with the 07.40 Euston to Pwllheli on 26th September 1987.

John Hillmer

Harlech is one of the crossing places on the single line between Barmouth and Pwllheli. On 26th September 1987, two 'Sprinters' pass each other – on the left No. 150124 forming the 09.10 Dovey Junction to Pwllheli and on the right, No. 150104 being the 09.40 Pwlhelli to Birmingham New Street.

John Hillmer

Passing Barmouth Harbour on 26th September 1987, is a four-car train formed of 'Sprinter' Class 150/1 units with the 11.25 Pwllheli to Machynlleth.

John Hillmer

Class 37 Nos 37215 and 37029 pull away from Penrhyndeudraeth on 25th June 1988 with 1J19, the 07.40 Euston to Pwllheli, "The Snowdonian". Both locomotives were based at Tinsley and belonged to the Freight Sector.

John Hillmer

Crossing the Afon Dwyryd, between Penrhyndeudraeth and Llandecwyn, on 25th June 1988, Class 150/1 No. 150104 forms the 13.13 Pwllheli to Machynlleth.

John Hillmer

'Sprinter' unit No. 150134 makes a call at Porthmadog station on 6th April 1988, forming the 11.25 departure from Pwllheli to Machynlleth. Porthmadog is one of the four intermediate crossing places on the single line between Dovey Junction and Pwllheli.

Paul Shannon

The much-reduced Pwllheli terminus on 6th April 1988, showing 'Sprinter' unit No. 150134 standing at the one remaining platform, after working the 08.20 service from Machynlleth. The building on the right is part of a supermarket which has been constructed on former railway land.

Paul Shannon

About half a mile north of the closed Pontdolgoch station, on the descent from Talerddig, English Electric Co-Co No. D6984 (subsequently to become Class 37 No. 37274) heads the 14.55 Aberystwyth to Manchester Piccadilly on 25th June 1966.

Michael Mensing

◁

Class 24 No. 5092 shunts the pick-up goods at Pwllheli East yard on 28th March 1973. There has been no revenue-earning freight on the Dovey Junction to Pwllheli section of the Cambrian since the temporary closure of Barmouth Bridge.

Wyn Hobson

▷

Class 24 No. 5085 shunts gunpowder vans at Penrhyndeudraeth on 7th September 1971. After the temporary closure of Barmouth Bridge, the explosives were taken by road to Blaenau Ffestiniog goods depot for distribution by rail, and then in 1985 a new private siding was opened for the traffic at Maentwrog Road, just short of Trawsfynydd. By mid-1988, however, the level of traffic had declined considerably and was expected to cease completely by the end of the year.

Wyn Hobson

The 12.30 Aberystwyth to Shrewsbury, formed of a two-car Metro-Cammell diesel multiple unit, slows by Hookagate signal box near Shrewsbury on Saturday 23rd April 1966, in order to give up the single line token.

Michael Mensing

Passing Croes Newydd old steam shed on 11th October 1974, Class 47 No. 47462 approaches North Fork crossing and Wrexham General station. The ex-GWR depot was of the roundhouse type and remained open until March 1967, although diesel locomotives were stabled nearby for many years afterwards. The building was subsequently demolished.

John Hillmer

On 26th August 1966, Class 108 diese multiple units are seen at Cheste Northgate. This ex-Cheshire Line Committee station closed in 1969 wit services being concentrated at Genera Northgate's connection with North Wale was its services to Shotton (High Leve with some trains going through t Wrexham Central on this ex-LNER line.

John Marsha

Class 40 No. D232 *Empress of Canada* leaves Chester with the 07.14 Bangor to Euston on 2nd April 1971. The LNWR lower quadrant signals at this location were the last of their kind to survive in quantity on BR.

Wyn Hobson